# A NEW AND POWERFUL YOU

Empowering ideas for the body, mind, and spirit

by Brenda Lea

Copyright © 2020 by Brenda Fisher

All rights reserved. No part of this publication may be reproduced, distributed, or transmitted in any form or by any means, including photocopying, recording, or other electronic or mechanical methods, without the prior written permission of the publisher, except in the case brief quotations embodied in critical reviews and certain other noncommercial uses permitted by the copyright law. For permission requests, e-mail to the address below.

brenda@anewandpowerfulyou.com
ANewAndPowerfulYou.com

Editing by Sofia Dutczak and Stephanie Raupp
Cover and interior book design by LTCMedia

ISBN: 978-0-578-64313-7 (Paperback)
ISBN: 978-0-578-64314-4 (E-book)

Printed in the United States of America

Brenda Lea Publishing

## Contents

Acknowledgments .................................................................. 4
Introduction ........................................................................... 5

Chapter 1 - Our Body and Our Life ................................... 9

Chapter 2 - Stress Management
for the Body and Mind ...................................................... 19

Chapter 3 - Confidence and Self-esteem:
Changing our Beliefs ......................................................... 23

Chapter 4 - How to Break the Barrier ............................. 29

Chapter 5 - Forgiveness ..................................................... 43

Chapter 6 - Why ................................................................... 49

Chapter 7 - Grief ................................................................. 53

Chapter 8 - Dark Night of the Soul ................................. 57

Chapter 9 - Spirituality ..................................................... 61

Chapter 10 - An Interview with
Dr. Roger on Spirituality .................................................. 65

Chapter 11 - My Journey Back Home ............................. 75

Chapter 12 - The Power of Prayer and Faith ................ 79

Chapter 13 - An Interview with Courtney Smith:
Tips on How to be Successful .......................................... 83

Chapter 14 - Meditation:
My Healing of the Body Meditation .............................. 93

# Acknowledgments

I would like to dedicate this book to my parents, without them, this book would never have been possible. My mother has been my lifelong rock and my best friend. Although my father is no longer on this earthly plane, I know he is always beside me and is proud of my accomplishments. Thank you both, I love you with all my heart!

I want to give a special thanks to Dr. Roger Teel, Dr. Erin Foley, and Courtney Smith for letting me interview them and include their interviews in this book.

I give a warm thanks to Sofia Dutczak and Stephanie Raupp for their editing and to Keren Kilgore for consulting with me on the publishing of this book. I also want to acknowledge Ernest Purisima for the photo of me on the back of the book and Tammy Johnson for the logo.

I want to thank Mile Hi Church and all the beautiful souls that helped me become the person I am today.

# Introduction

## BODY and MIND and SPIRIT

*Life is a mirror and will reflect back to the thinker what he thinks into it.*

~Ernest Holmes

    The three parts of us-Body, Mind, and Spirit-are what I believe make up our being. If one or all of these are out of sync, it can cause disharmony in us.
    This is a book written for you and your future journeys, but it is also about my soul journey. I earned my education through life's journeys and experiences, and I want to share it with you.
    This is a book about empowerment. There are a lot of different things we can do that can help our body, mind, and spirit to be healthy. I will give ideas on how to help you overcome challenges and empower yourself.

We all have our challenges to overcome. Life is about the journey to the top of the mountain and not about staying on the top. I have faced many challenges, and that is what has driven me to write this book. I want to help people and give them some ways they can empower themselves and overcome life challenges.

Some of the challenges I have faced include my ex-husband taking my 4-year-old son away after I told him I wanted a divorce. I only saw my son twice in 5 years. He harassed me to no end until my son was grown. My fiancé, who was the father of my daughter, was murdered. I lost my first and only grandchild to SIDS when he was 5 months old. Most of my life, I have struggled with allergies, asthma, eczema, and alopecia, which are all autoimmune diseases. Alopecia attacks the hair follicles, so as a result, I have lost all my hair, and it has not come back after 10 years.

I will tell my stories for each of these events and trials in the following chapters. Even though there have been more challenges, I never gave up! I never lost hope that things will and can get better. I found strength deep inside, and that is the strength we all have inside us. I used that strength to keep me going. If we set limitations on ourselves, we can never grow beyond those. We need to keep striving for higher goals and dreams.

I know you must be strong, too, or you would not be reading this book. You are looking for a way to better yourself. You can do it! I believe in you!

In the end, it all comes down to you and your willingness to make a change for a new and powerful you and a better life for yourself. I will be giving you tools, but only you can decide if you want to use them or if they are a fit for you. I want to make a difference in your life and help you overcome challenges and empower yourself.

In this book, I will express my ideas and opinions on spirituality. I have also interviewed someone who helped me with my spirituality. Because this is a controversial subject, I hope you will take what works for you and disregard what doesn't work for you, without judgment. I don't have all the answers regarding spirituality and don't claim to be a religious expert.

There is a very specific reason I chose to put the dragonfly on the cover of this book. I was working in downtown Denver, and my workspace was a cubicle near a window on the 41$^{st}$ floor of a skyscraper. I came out of a meeting with my manager, and we had not seen eye to eye on some things. I was feeling upset. As I went back to my cubicle, I looked outside the window. Forty-one stories up in the air and outside my window was a big dragonfly. I knew it was there to give me a message. I found that in some cultures, the dragonfly is the symbol of a warrior. I believe it was trying to tell me to stay strong and be a new and powerful person.

So, are you ready to dive in and see where this book can take you?

# A New and Powerful You

# Chapter 1
# Our Body and Our Life

*But the real secret to lifelong good health is actually the opposite:
Let your body take care of you.*
~Deepak Chopra

Our physical body is very important. Without it, we would not be having our human experience. Our body is energy, and it carries our life force.

What if we treated our body like we would want someone else to treat us? When I was in my twenties and thirties, I never thought about treating my body the way I should have. I was a heavy smoker, and my diet sucked. I never had to worry about exercise until I hit about 40, and my weight became a problem. I had to learn to exercise and eat healthy.

I quit smoking after being a smoker for 29 years. I was 43 years old, and it was one of the hardest things I have ever done. After trying numerous times and trying many products,

I quit cold turkey. I had tried the Nicorette gum, the nicotine patch, and even hypnosis, but none of them worked. I had sinus surgery to remove a polyp. After that surgery, I imagined that if I smoked, I would be pouring nasty tar into the open wound in my sinus cavity. This was enough of a visual to gross me out and keep me from smoking. I imagined that if I smoke, the new cells could become abnormal cells. Sinus cancer did not sound pleasant. The fear of getting to the place of no return, specifically lung cancer, and leaving my children behind or suffering from a long-term illness because of smoking helped me quit. One thing which really motivated me to quit was this thought; if I truly love myself, I would not be doing something that hurts me, such as smoking.

What we do to our bodies now can affect us down the road. If we drink sodas every day, we can become overweight and eventually get diabetes. Because it hasn't happened yet, we don't always see the long-term effects. If we keep doing unhealthy things and then we get down the road, there can become a point of no return – which we never want to reach.

I try to envision when I'm doing healthy things like working out at the gym, that when I'm 70, I can have the strength and stamina to do the things I love. I want to travel around the world and feel strong, not weak, and sickly. I want to continue to teach Tai Chi classes and be an inspiration for other seniors when I'm a senior. I don't look at the short term; but rather the long-term effect of how I eat and exercise today.

I have interviewed Dr. Erin Foley about some tips for being healthy and ways we can channel our energy for better health. I think you will enjoy what she has to say. Some of the things we can do to make us healthier can even be fun.

Dr. Foley has been practicing natural health care for about 30 years. It has been her life work. She is a doctor of chiropractic, acupuncture, and functional medicine. She started gaining her

## Chapter 1- Our Body and Our Life

knowledge at 20 when she started working for a chiropractor. Her favorite place to hang out was a health food store, and she learned about natural ways to take care of the body without drugs and surgery. She became a chiropractor and has always had a desire to keep learning, so she went on to learn acupuncture in 2000. She also took classes in allergy elimination techniques, or NAET, and in 2014 became a functional medicine practitioner. She has a lot of her patients who thank her for helping them become healthier and avoiding unnecessary surgery and drugs.

I asked Dr. Erin Foley to explain to us how our body is energy and what are the ways in which we can regulate our energy or Chi so we can feel better. Her response was:

> *From an Eastern standpoint, the Chi is basically the energy that runs through the acupuncture meridians in our bodies, and it is accessed by the acupuncture points. It is a form of electrical energy that you can't see, but Chi can become stagnant, like a stagnant pool of water. When it is stuck, it can become excessive – too much energy or deficient energy. I recommend acupuncture for regulating your Chi. You don't necessarily have to have pain or illness; you can balance your energy with acupuncture or Chinese herbs and exercises like Tai Chi and qigong. Those are the classic ways of regulating your Chi. From a Western standpoint of view, the Chi is the adrenal glands. Most women I see that have a hormone imbalance, there is an underlining deficiency of the adrenal glands and adrenal fatigue, which can be because of a lifestyle issue. There are many ways to improve your health by improving your adrenals.*

I did some research on the adrenal glands so it could help you understand what they are. The adrenal glands are small glands located on top of each kidney. They produce a variety of hormones, including adrenaline and the steroids aldosterone and cortisol. Hormones that you can't live without, including sex hormones and cortisol. Cortisol helps you respond to stress and has many other important functions. With adrenal glands disorders, your glands make too much or not enough hormones.

To help support healthy adrenal glands, doctors recommend a diet of protein, healthy fats, and nutrient-dense carbohydrates. Include vegetables to get the vitamins your body needs. Adrenal fatigue is linked to intense stress or recovery from a serious illness like flu or pneumonia. Finding ways to reduce stress in our lives will help. Tai' Chi and acupressure or acupuncture certainly help as well. I asked Dr. Foley what are some fun ways can keep the body healthy. She responded;

> *This is a fun question. What we need to do is get out of the thought of what should I do for my body. Instead, ask our body the question, 'what do you want, body?' We are usually in our head all the time instead of in our bodies, which is a natural way of being in our Western Society. So, instead, get in touch with what is fun for your body. Me personally, I enjoy Epsom salt baths, yoga, and Pilates, and my body loves hiking and skiing in the mountains, massages, sex, and sleep. Those are some examples for me. I don't like going to a gym and getting on the treadmill or lifting weights, it is not fun for my body, it usually hurts me, so I don't do it. Instead, I ask my body, 'what do you want to do, body?' That is the biggest question you can ask to find out what you want to do with your body moving forward. Ask your body: 'What do you require? Ask yourself: Do you like massages? Do you like acupuncture? What do you like to do?'*

# Chapter 1- Our Body and Our Life

I personally like to go to the gym and get on the treadmill, get a monthly massage, do Tai Chi, walk my dog, and take long hot showers. Just do what feels right for your body. Do something fun that gets your body moving. There are so many options out there like swimming, hiking with friends, walking, skiing, biking, running, and so many more that can be fun.

Dr. Foley also says, "Sleep is so important because sleep is absolutely necessary for good health. It is not an option. When you sleep, and you get good sleep, you feel better, and your health is better."

I sleep nine to ten hours a night because that is what my body requires to stay healthy and keep my autoimmune in check. If I don't get adequate sleep, I will get run down. My autoimmune kicks in, and I can get very sick. Dr. Foley says;

*Be kind to your body and stop judging your body. There are no shoulds about what we should do with our bodies, they just are. We may think, "I should go to the gym four days a week," for example, but if your body doesn't like that, there is a high chance you may become injured. Be kind and stop any judgment you have of your body. Find out from your body what is fun for your body, what it wants to do, what it requires. Do things that light you up. Don't do what you think you "should be" doing due to external pressures. When it comes to food and your hunger level, ask your body what you require at the moment. Maybe your body really wants a drink of water or wants to go for a walk.*

*It doesn't have to be all drudgery. Nor does your diet. Ask your body, 'What is fun, what do you crave'? Don't eat things you hate. An example would be if you hate Brussels sprouts, don't eat them because your reaction is your body telling you it doesn't want to eat that. We can be disconnected, all in our heads and separate from our bodies, and think that we should eat this and do that because everyone else does.*

The next question I asked Dr. Foley was, "What are some things a person could do to maintain optimal health now and things that they can do to keep themselves healthy in their future?"

She said, "Everything we do now and has done affects our future health. You can eat badly and do a lot of things to your body when you're younger that you can't do as you get older. What we do in our forties will affect us in our fifties and sixties. It's better to be taking care of your body, like taking care of your car. If you take care of it, you will have a better aging. For me, I go back to fun ways to take care of my body and what it wants." Dr. Foley goes on to say;

*One of the things I feel very strongly about is that one of the big drivers of disease is inflammation, and that is well proven by research. Inflammation underlies in diabetes, heart disease, and cancer. And what drives inflammation is a high insulin and blood sugar level, and that is something you can actively do to take care of every day with your diet. You can also check your blood. You can do a blood test for fasting blood glucose level A1C and get a baseline because diabetes 2 doesn't happen overnight; it takes time to build up. And if you only see your doctor once a year, it may get under the radar, and you could be pre-diabetic for a while, but you can also test yourself at home with a glucose tester. That is my do-it-yourself solution. You can test your own blood sugar levels, and you can see how you respond to foods by fasting in the morning and then testing two hours after food and see if you are eating too many sugars or refined carbs.*

## Chapter 1- Our Body and Our Life

*Our food pyramid in this county is based on a low fat, high carbohydrate diet, and that diet will cause inflammation, which causes diabetes and heart disease and cancer. So, what I recommend to all my patients is 3 different versions of low-carbohydrate diets. There is the Dr. Adkins diet or a Paleo or Ketogenic diet. These are practical tips to keep yourself healthy and lower your inflammation.*

To sum up, what Dr. Foley has to say is that we need to take care of our bodies and ask our body what it wants in order to stay healthy. We need to eat healthy, move our body, and get good sleep. We have so many options for healthy foods and fun things to do.

Please, for the sake of your health and wellbeing, always check with your doctor before starting a new diet or making any drastic changes in eating habits or exercise.

Our Western society is focused on medication and surgery. If you feel that is what you require, please follow what your doctor wants you to do. But we could also avoid some medications and surgeries by following a good diet.

We need to take care of our body now, so we don't get to the point of surgeries and medications. This is the only body we have!

One important way to reduce the inflammation in our bodies is correcting our diets. There are a lot of diets out there to choose from. I personally count calories and eat healthy meats such as chicken, fish, and bison. I eat fresh vegetables and fruits and avoid eating processed foods for the most part.

For someone else, it could be the Paleo diet or another diet. I say 'diet,' but it must be a lifestyle change, not just a way of eating. Once we go off the diet, we can go right back to our old eating habits, which can then bring us back to inflammation and weight gain, which we want to avoid.

Sugar can really wreak havoc on the body. It can cause weight gain, blood sugar problems, heart disease, and many other issues. There are also debates about artificial sweeteners and if they are good for you or not. I personally use Pure Monk Fruit, which you can order on Amazon. I like Monk Fruit because it has no calories and is a natural sweetener, not artificial. Our bodies need a balance of proper sleep, exercise, and food. We also need to make sure we stay hydrated with lots of clean water. Be good to your body, and thank your body for supporting you in your daily life.

As Dr. Foley mentioned, our bodies are made up of energy meridians, which are energy highways through our body. We can't see the meridians, but sometimes these meridians can be blocked. Blockages in this system may be caused by stress, injury, bad diet, or addictions to alcohol or drugs. These blockages can cause health issues. Some of the ways to unblock these is to do acupuncture, acupressure, qigong or tai chi. There are also different types of energy healing, one I would recommend is reiki.

There are a lot of choices to keep our body healthy, pick the ones that work the best for you. Eating healthy is important as it could give you more energy and keep you from getting certain diseases. I think you will feel a lot better if you avoid processed foods, eat more fruits and vegetables and fresh meats. Processed foods are more convenient but full of chemicals and wasted calories. Think of processed food as dead food because all the living "good stuff" has been taken out. Processed foods are not good for the body and can cause weight gain and fatigue.

## Chapter 1- Our Body and Our Life

Some of my eating healthy tips:
- Fill up on fiber and protein
- Cut back on sugar
- Add calcium and magnesium for bone health
- Cook meals at home. When you make it yourself; you can better control what you are eating and how it is prepared.
- Eat in moderation

# Chapter 2
## Stress Management for the Body and Mind

*Prepare your mind to receive the best that life has to offer.*
*~Ernest Holmes*

Stress is one of the things we need to get under control and manage. Stress causes havoc in the body and mind. Stress can keep us awake at night and cause disease in the body.

At one point, I had been telling everyone, including myself, that my job was *not* stressful and that I was happy, and it was true. Then they decided at my job to add a new piece to my workload, and it became overwhelming. I was completely stressed over it. I thought to myself, 'what is going on here? I set up my life circumstances, and my intentions are to not be stressed, so why has it changed from not being stressful to being stressful?' I realized that I, myself, was making it stressful. I needed to step back and see that I could only do what I could do. I was not going to let this added step at work stress me, but just do what I can do in a day and not worry or stress over what I didn't get done. Tomorrow is a new day. Sometimes we can get ourselves worked up over things we don't have control over and need to realize that we ourselves are making the circumstance stressful. The greatest thing that happened was when I let it go, they hired someone to take over that extra workload, and I was no longer overwhelmed.

There are many things we can do to manage stress. Breath is one of the most important things in life. Without breath, there is no life. When we are having a stressful day, we need to think about our breath. When we are stressed, we tend to hold our breath. Instead, we need to take a minute and take three deep breaths to get the oxygen flowing into our blood and brains. I suggest box breathing, also known as a 4-sided breath. To do this, you breathe in for a count of 4, hold for a count of 4 and exhale for a count of 4.

Meditation is a great way to de-stress. It calms the mind and body and helps to ground us and keep us centered. During the day at work, you may want to take a 10-minute break in the middle of your day and meditate. Some people feel like they can't sit still long enough for a meditation, but even 10 minutes can really help with stress reduction. 20 minutes or more is what I suggest for the best results. Sit or lay down, close your eyes, concentrate on your breath, and focus on relaxing. If you have never done meditation before, I do have a short meditation example in Chapter 14. Meditation is basically relaxing and letting go of stress and thoughts.

I find that exercise is great for stress management as it gets the blood flowing and can help you sleep better and have more energy during the day. Walking can be a great and easy exercise for most. Even if you walk slowly for 30 minutes a day, it can be a great benefit for your body. You may want to join a health club as they offer different types of classes for different types of exercise.

One of my favorite activities I do to relieve stress is tai chi. I'm an accredited instructor in T'ai Chi Chih and T'ai Chi: Moving for Better Balance and I teach classes. Tai chi moves the life force

## Chapter 2 - Stress Management for the Body and Mind

energy through the meridians and unblocks stuck energy. It is great for stress relief and gives people more energy. People who do tai chi on a regular basis are a lot healthier as it has proven to help with balance and build stronger bones. My students will tell me how much it has helped them in so many ways. Many have said it helps with their balance, bone density results went up, helps to deal with chemo treatments and stress.

Tai Chi tends to help most people in areas where they need help the most, like lowering blood pressure, sense of peace, bone density improving, and more. The practice focuses on where you need the most physical benefit. A lot of people enjoy yoga, which is very beneficial for the body. Some of the benefits of yoga are increased flexibility, increased muscle strength and tone, and more energy. Remember, it is important to do whatever you enjoy. Whether it is yoga, snowboarding, or swimming, do what makes you happy.

Sleep is very important, but sometimes stress can lead to insomnia. Research has linked insomnia to many health issues like high blood pressure, diabetes, and congestive heart failure. Herbal remedies can help with insomnia, but you should always talk to your doctor before doing them. Some people like to listen to soothing music, which can help put them to sleep. Doing the 4-sided breath can help you drift off to sleep and quiet the mind. Sometimes I will wake up and go over something that is bothering me repeatedly in my head. I do the 4-sided breath, and it takes my mind off my worries. I would also suggest not have a television in your bedroom – the bedroom is for sleep.

I personally suffer from allergies and alopecia, which are both autoimmune disorders. I have noticed I feel a lot better when I eat health-consciously, and my body suffers when I don't. I teach Tai Chi and do meditation in my classes. While doing these things, I look at how I'm handling stress and what I can do differently to improve.

Your body is the only one you will have for your whole lifetime. You will need to take care of it. If we treat our body like it was our best friend, who we care deeply about, and would do anything for, we would be happier and healthier. Thank your body for supporting you no matter what condition it is, as it allows you to experience this life.

Stress cannot be managed out of our existence, so we need to do the best to maintain it. To reduce stress, we need to look at the stress in our lives and see if we are the ones causing it. We may need to stop putting so much pressure on ourselves. It is important to create an existence that reduces as much stress as we can and plans for expected stressors. Remember, meditation, Tai Chi, yoga, or exercise can all be great stress relievers. Other things that are important are getting enough sleep (and taking the steps for you to get good sleep) and eating healthy to keep the body alert and focused.

Above all, remember to love yourself!

## Chapter 3
## Confidence and Self-esteem:
## Changing our Beliefs

*You never know how strong you are
until being strong is your only choice.*
*-Bob Marley*

Our self-esteem and confidence are a big determining factor in our lives. A lot of our self-esteem issues and ideas that keep us from our true potential came from the beliefs we got from our childhood. One example may be that the child who felt unsafe or unloved can follow the pattern of the parent and make their children feel unloved or unsafe or break the chain and turn the bad experience into motivation to be better than their parents. There are so many stories of successful people who had a horrible childhood but overcame it and became successful.

Sometimes we can get caught up in the victim mode. We could blame people and circumstances from the past for our fears and shortcomings and the reasons we fail today. But the past is the past, and once we decide to stop being the victim, we can change our life. We are the only one who can change our ideas and beliefs. If you want to change your life, you need to change your way of thinking.

Once you make the decision to stop being a victim to circumstances, you will see a big change in your life; but you must take that first step. For example, when you constantly say that you don't have money or you can't afford to do things, that becomes your reality. You will never have the money because you are putting this belief out into the universe. The universe can give us what we declare to be true. If you want more money, then you need to stop saying you don't have enough money. You need to believe you have money now, even if you don't have it yet. Sometimes we must step out in faith and just believe. It is the law of attraction.

When we are working through something challenging in our lives, our feelings are different than when we are at a content place. Celebrate the challenges! The challenges can mean we are in a place where we are going to make better changes in our life, even if it doesn't seem that way at the time.

Our perceptions can be different at different times of our life as we grow and change over time. I have noticed as I reach my fifties that in all the different stages in my life, I was growing, mentally, physically, spiritually, into who I am now. Who I was at twenty or thirty is not who I am today, but the experiences I had during those times shaped me into the person I'm today.

I want to share my example of learning to accept something that I wasn't prepared to accept and how it has made me stronger. One of my greatest challenges is having alopecia. Alopecia is an autoimmune disorder that affects the hair and results in sudden hair loss. I now live with being bald every day - which is a real struggle as a woman. There is nothing I can do about it but accept it.

## Chapter 3 - Confidence and Self Esteem

There is no cure for alopecia, and though stress may worsen the condition, what causes a person to experience this disorder is unknown.

When I was younger, I had beautiful blonde hair. My hair was my pride and joy. Ever since I was a teenager, I loved my hair and would spend hours styling it. I find it ironic that I lost something that was so important to me, and I had to learn to live without it. The first time I experienced the effects of alopecia was when I was dating my second husband, which should have been a clue to not marry him. I was 25 years old. I had recently left my first marriage and had a new baby and was not ready to be committed to someone else. I tried numerous times to break it off with him, but he would hound me until I gave in. I was young and naïve, like the saying, "If I only knew then what I know now." Luckily, my hair grew back. For the next 24 years, I had no more issues with my alopecia.

That is until I got a new manager who hounded me constantly and would make my life a living hell while I was at work. He seemed to hate me, and I didn't understand why at the time. I had been at that company for six years before he arrived and loved my job. The company paid well, had retirement benefits, and had many other awesome perks. Unfortunately, the stress of working under this manager caused my hair to start falling out. At first, it was just on the sides of my head, and I was able to cover it up by styling my hair differently. I went to a dermatologist and got steroid injections in my scalp. Three different times I went in for this treatment, which consisted of about 50 needle pricks on my scalp. It was incredibly painful. I would have a blasting headache after each treatment. I tried steroid creams as well, but nothing worked. Instead, I started looking for wigs.

I left the company after 10 years and moved to another town for a fresh start. About a month after I left, I lost all of the hair on my head. It was devastating and heartbreaking to wash my hair as it would come out in clumps in the shower. I tried to be strong and soldier through it. Then one day, I looked in the mirror, and I noticed that half of one of my eyebrows was gone, and I lost it. I broke down, and I cried and cried. I called my Mom, and she comforted me as best she could. She told me it would be alright, and I could pencil my eyebrows in, but in that moment, I felt so lost. It felt like no one could ever understand the incredible sense of loss I was feeling.

Then I lost my eyelashes. I cried a lot and grieved over the loss of my hair. It had always been a part of my identity – now it was gone. It felt like I had lost a part of myself.

I went to an alopecia support group, but it wasn't as helpful as I hoped. Some of the people in the group were having a harder time coping with Alopecia even more than I was. It was heartbreaking and depressing to see other women in so much pain. Some were afraid to leave their home because of what people would think. Others would not take their wig off, even in the privacy of their home.

I came to realize that this was a lesson I needed to learn, and its message was one I needed to embrace. I am beautiful inside, and it took losing my hair to fully understand this. Outer beauty will someday fade, but inner beauty will stay strong. I have connected with my inner beauty. I don't go out in public with my bald head showing, but I do go out with a wig or bandana. When I wear a bandana, I occasionally get people who will approach me and ask how long – thinking I have cancer. I used to say I have alopecia, but now I just smile and don't let it get to me. I am not on the dating scene anymore, and I have decided to believe that God someday will bring me the right person who will love me for my inner beauty. If not, I love being with me.

Knowing that people are afraid to go out in public because of their alopecia or other issues makes me sad. I hope that people like me will inspire others to not let something like hair loss keep

## Chapter 3 - Confidence and Self Esteem

them from living their life to the fullest. It doesn't matter what others think. I go to the pool with my bandana on. When I get funny looks from people, it doesn't bother me because I'm not letting my alopecia control me or stop me from enjoying my life. I'm not going to hide in my house because I don't have hair. I put a wig on, pencil in my eyebrows, and go. Since I have lost my hair, I have become an accredited tai chi instructor, traveled around the world, and published this book. I have enough confidence to not let alopecia stand in my way.

You don't need someone else to validate your self-worth. Sometimes it is important to look at your situation with a sense of humor. As the saying goes, "it is better to laugh than cry." Life is too short to be miserable. I miss my beautiful hair, and I wish it would grow back. But the reality is, I must accept I may never get my hair back. All that matters is that I love myself, and I'm happy with who I am. I hope you will not let your imperfections keep you from enjoying your life to the fullest, either.

Love yourself no matter what your circumstances may be. Don't let someone else try to put a standard on how you should be. You are important, and you do matter! You are one of a kind, there is no one out there like you. You are a unique spiritual treasure here to share with others what only you can share.

## Chapter 4
## How to Break the Barrier

*God gives some more than others
because some accept more than others.*
~Ernest Holmes

The barrier is a place where we can get stuck and not move forward because of unconscious thoughts or beliefs.

As young children, our brains are like sponges that soak up everything around us. We don't yet have the critical thinking skills to decide if the thoughts, ideas, and beliefs we get from others will serve us well. We get these from our parents and other family members, our teachers, and the media. As we get older, all these thoughts and emotions become buried in our subconscious mind. Our conscious thoughts are our thinking thoughts; our subconscious thoughts are what can cause us the behaviors we sometimes don't understand.

Have you ever wondered why you are always doing something repeatedly even though consciously you know you should not or don't want to be doing it again? Where do our bad habits come from? For example, let's say you struggle in relationships. You really want to do better in your relationships, but you always seem to pick the wrong person and end up getting hurt all over again. You realize it is the same type of person, just different packaging.

There is some belief in you, on a subconscious level, that keeps you going back to the same type of person in romantic relationships. In order to break through this mental barrier and choose someone different in the next relationship, you need to decide what you really want in a healthy, loving relationship. For example, someone who is caring and who enjoys the same things you like.

Write down all that you want in this relationship and the things you want to change. Then close your eyes and feel and imagine the situation or person as you want things to be. Do this three times a day for ten to twenty minutes. This will allow these thoughts to reach the subconscious level so you can change your situation. Then every hour, read what it is you want to change. Even better, take the time to write it down again every day. You may have even heard of a vision board. On a vision board, you place pictures of the items you want in your life. Or you can write down the emotions you want to feel, as an example, more peace or joy.

I know that visualization like this works. When I was in my twenties, I wanted to live on a million-dollar ranch. I wrote down what I wanted and imagined it every day. Eventually, I did live on a million-dollar ranch. It may have not been exactly what I had hoped for, but it did happen.

If you want to get through this barrier, sometimes you need to take an action that you really want to do but are afraid. Our subconscious wants us to feel safe, so we may end up thinking, "don't do it; you might fail." You may start thinking the kind of thoughts that can keep you from your full potential. Our

# Chapter 4 - How to Break the Barrier

behavior is driven by the subconscious mind. Everyday tasks are performed via the conscious mind, but most actions will depend on the subconscious mind. When the subconscious mind takes control, your conscious mind is unaware you acted upon the subconscious. Sometimes when there is something you're afraid to do, you should think about doing it because if it isn't something you are a little afraid of, you are probably not reaching outside the barrier.

As a single mother, I had never bought a house. Renting had always been the best option for me. After renting for my whole life, I bought a duplex for my Mom and myself so that she could live next door to me. I was terrified to make such a big commitment. I almost backed out, and I lost a lot of sleep over the stress of going through the home buying process. Now, I look at the house market today, and I think it was one of the smartest things I did. If I had let my fears win, I would have not bought the duplex. If I had not bought the duplex, I would not be able to afford the increase of rent prices in Colorado at this time. Getting past my fear paid off.

Don't let fear keep you from possibly having one of the best experiences you could ever have. I'm afraid of flying, but I still get on a plane. If I had not overcome this fear, I would have missed out on some wonderful trips abroad to places like Italy, Ireland, and Scotland. I try to remind myself when I fly that only I make up the beliefs that make flying scary to me. I tell myself in the moment that I am on a plane, which is a fact, but I am not in danger. Even when there is turbulence, I remind myself that the plane is still up in the air, and all is okay.

I was afraid to write this next story because I was afraid some people would judge me for my decisions. I decided to not let this fear keep me from telling this story. If I can help even one person by telling my story, it is worth it to me. I was afraid to leave my second marriage. I was afraid to be alone, terrified that I couldn't survive on my own and support my children. I was young and didn't have a lot of working experience. At that point, the jobs I had included being a cashier at a convenience store, ride operator at an amusement park, and working a paper route; but none would pay a lot of money.

John, which is not his real name, was controlling. He didn't want me to leave the house unless I had the children with me. He would get drunk and fight with me. He would lock me in the bedroom. He would pick me up and pin me against the wall. It was awful. He threatened that if I ever left, he would take my children from me.

If I tried to push back, he would drag the children into the argument and say, "See kids your mom is having a tantrum," then start laughing.

I remember when I was four months pregnant with our only child, I got appendicitis. After the surgery to remove my appendix, I got pneumonia. The baby survived even though the doctors told me I could possibly lose my child. At the time, this surgery was not laparoscopic; every cough was painful due to the 4-inch incision from the surgery. I was very sick. A family friend dropped by and asked if there was anything she could do to help me. I needed rest. I asked if she could take my 2 1/2-year-old from my first marriage to daycare in the morning. I would have had to walk him there because John didn't want me to have a car when he wasn't home.

John pulled me aside and said, "Can I talk to you?" He took me in the other room and said, "Who do you think you are? Telling people what to do?" I started to cry and replied that she asked me what she could do to help. I told the friend what he said, and she became incredibly upset. She told him that she offered and would be there in the morning to pick up the child. He was so cruel, wanting me to walk my son a mile to daycare with pneumonia, a painful incision, and pregnant too. He had

## Chapter 4 - How to Break the Barrier

no compassion for what I was going through. I would try to talk to him, but he would not listen to me. The mental abuse was horrible.

I would go to church with a girlfriend on Sundays. We would take our children and afterwards get coffee and doughnuts. When I came home, John would accuse me of cheating on him. After a while, I gave up spending time with my girlfriends. I never once cheated on him while we were together. We went to marriage counseling, and I told the marriage counselor that he needed to change, or I would leave him. I put a 6-month time limit on our relationship. The marriage counselor asked John what he thought about what I had said, and he said, "I don't care what she wants, I'm not going to change anything."

He decided we would move to a million-dollar ranch in the middle of nowhere in Moffat county in Colorado and rent out our house in the Colorado Springs area. He got this idea from a friend. The plan was that we would remodel the ranch house and tend to the sheep. The man, who was buying the ranch, would then pay us to live there and supply everything we needed. Worried that things may not go according to plan, I asked my husband to get a contract that stated this man would take care of us as long as we took care of the property and sheep. He said it was okay not to have a contract and that we didn't need to worry. We rented out our home on a one-year lease and moved there.

For the first couple of months, everything was good. But then the man wasn't sure he was going to buy the ranch, after all, so he quit sending us money. We had no money for food or heat. and life was miserable. John was hunting grouse and wild rabbit so we could eat. We had nothing else, no vegetables or bread, just meat to eat. There we were, in the middle of winter, stuck in this ranch house. At Christmas, we had no money for gifts for the two little children.

The town was very small, and they heard about our situation, so they got us some propane for heat and groceries at the little convenience store in town and gifts for Christmas.

I decided after that, it was the last straw for me, and for that marriage. My fear of leaving him was smaller than my fear of living with him in this situation. It was January of 1990, and my parents had just moved to Nevada. I was beyond frustrated with the situation, so I called my mom. I told her I was so depressed. It had gotten to the point of me wanting to take my life or leave him, but I had to do something. My mom said, "Pack up the kids and come here." At the time, we only had one vehicle, so I put the children in the truck, and we hit the road for Laughlin, Nevada.

My plan was to file for divorce and give him joint custody of our child. He begged me to come back to him and said he would change. But I knew after 7 years, those were lies and he wasn't going to change. I had moved into a place in Arizona with the help of my parents and the Salvation Army. I got a job at a convenience store and was able to get the kids in daycare.

I was getting on my feet and looking into legal aid to file for the divorce. I had even started dating and met the man who would later become my fiancé and the father of my daughter.

One day, John showed up. He was living somewhere close to Colorado Springs, Colorado, and said he wanted to take our child to the store to get him a pair of new shoes. I was feeling sick that day, I had just found out that I was pregnant with my daughter, and so I agreed to let him take him. This was a decision I will regret for the rest of my life. Instead of a quick trip to the shoe store, he took my son back to Colorado with him. He was only four years old and was a total momma's boy. I was frantic.

I called the legal aid, and a lawyer told me that if I wanted custody, I would need to have him back in Arizona before I filed anything. My sister and I went to Colorado to try to get him back.

## Chapter 4 - How to Break the Barrier

We asked around to find out where he was, but, unfortunately, I asked the wrong person. I ended up asking the woman who had been babysitting my son. She told John that I was there to get my son. He came up to the truck window and said, "So you want my son? You will never get him back."

I was so angry and heartbroken. I shouted, "I want my baby back!" I was screaming outside of the truck. The sheriff showed up, and he knew me because my dad had been in Search and Rescue. He asked me what was going on and I told him.

The whole time, John stood there, smirking. The Sherriff asked where the child was, and he replied, "I'm not telling you." The Sheriff apologized to me. Because we were legally married, he couldn't help me.

I went to social services, and they told me the same thing – we both had legal rights. If he wanted to keep him away from me, he could. I would have to file for divorce and get legal rights for custody. John did agree to let me see my son but only with other people around so I couldn't take him back to Arizona. My son was beside himself, he was so upset and kept saying, "I want to be with my mommy." John made it clear that it wasn't going to happen. My son was walking back and forth between me and him – confused and distraught. I had a decision to make.

I thought of the story in the bible about the two women who went to King Solomon, and both claimed to be a child's mother. King Solomon said he would split the child in half so each could have half of the child. One woman said that would be fine, the other one said, "No, please, spare the child's life and let the other woman have the child." King Solomon knew who the real mother was because she was willing to give up the child to spare his life. 1 Kings 3:16-28. Because my son was stressed, I decided to leave him with his Dad.

Hopefully, not for long. But just long enough for me to try and figure out another way to get him back. I had my oldest child from my first marriage, who needed me and a baby on the way to think about as well.

I went back to Arizona without my beloved son. I cried my heart out all the way home and every night for two weeks straight and many more nights after that. I have never felt such an intense pain in my heart. I had this big hole in my life that nothing could fill. My oldest child was heartbroken without his little brother. Why did John have to be so cruel by keeping our son from his Mom and brother? I know he was angry I left, so he made sure everyone had to suffer. My oldest son told me that when I was not around, which was rarely the case, John would stuff him in a sleeping bag and tie the end shut, which terrified him. He was only a toddler at the time, and he said the more he screamed to be let out, the more John would laugh. He was a cruel man.

After I went back to Arizona, John refused to let me see my son, talk to him, or know where he was. If I wanted to get in contact with my son, I had to go through a mutual friend to get a message to him.

Times were tough for my children and me. I was making about $6 an hour, and I was not getting child support from my oldest child's father – my first husband. He had walked out of his life when he was two years old. Later I did find his dad when my son was around 10 years old, but he still refused to pay any child support. My youngest child's dad had been murdered, and we were getting a small amount from social security. We only had about $20 a week for food for the three of us. After about 5 years, I was finally able to get enough money together for a lawyer to file for the divorce and get visitation rights. Sadly, by this time, John had already convinced my son I had abandoned him and never wanted him. He also convinced the lawyers and the judge that I was a terrible mom who abandoned her child. I only got

## Chapter 4 - How to Break the Barrier

two weeks for visitation in a year. I had to pay child support even though he was making three times the amount I was, and I had two other children to support. I had to have all medical and dental insurance for our son and pay all transportation costs to see my son. To add insult to injury, he got the house and all the belongings. He threw away all my belongings instead of returning them. There were irreplaceable items I had from childhood and after.

I did get a stipulation clause that if I moved back to Colorado, I would get visitation of every other weekend. Every other holiday and two weeks in the summer. I moved back to Colorado permanently in 1998. Every other weekend, I would leave work on Friday. Drive 115 miles one-way to pick up my son and come back another 115 miles to my home. On Sunday, I take him back to his dad's. I put a lot of miles on my car, but to me, it was worth it. John refused to meet me halfway because, in the divorce papers, it said I had to pay for all transportation costs, so he made me drive up to his door. If, for some reason, I couldn't pick him up that weekend, like if there was a major snowstorm, he would get angry at me and say, "You wanted him every other weekend so you should have to make the drive anyway."

He could never get over the anger at me leaving. He used our son to punish me for leaving him. He was always looking for ways to hurt me. I know John thought that if he used our son as a pawn, he would get me to come back; I knew I could never go back to his abusive and controlling ways, no matter what.

This decision was one I have struggled with internally but one I had to make. I regretted the separation because I lost so many years with my son, but I also learned to become strong and never had to live in an abusive situation again. The fear of leaving him was real, but it didn't outweigh the abuse I received from him. I had to make a tough call. When we must make a tough call, and there is fear, we must do what is best at the time. One of the most important things I learned from leaving was that I could take care of and support myself and my children. I faced that fear head on, and we survived.

I have not been in an abusive relationship since and never will be again. My son and I have a great relationship today, and that is what matters most. I can't change the past or the decisions I made. But what I can do now is enjoy the moments I get to have with my son and the bond that we share.

One of the things that help me deal with my fears is my belief in Angels. I believe that they are always surrounding and protecting me. Every time I get in my car or a plane, I ask the angels to watch over me and protect me. I believe they are always protecting my home. Two passages that give me hope are "He will give his Angels charge of you to guard you in all ways," (Psalm 91.11) and "Behold, I send an Angel before thee, to keep thee in the way, and to bring thee into the place which I have prepared." (Exodus 23.20)

Faith is believing that everything will be okay. Even though we are not always conscious of it, we use faith in almost everything we do. For example, when you get in your car to drive to work, you have faith that you will get to work safely. If you leave the house to go to the grocery store, you trust you will get to the store and return home with your groceries. We live our lives in constant faith. Apply this faith in the moments that you are afraid.

Fear can create a victim mindset. For example, if you were robbed at gunpoint, it would be a very scary experience and would cause a lot of fear during that time. After the incident is over, you may go over and over it in your head. This can intensify what happened, which in turn could cause more stress and other fears. By replaying it in your head, your belief of what happened may become distorted, intensified, and increase your thinking as a victim. You might start thinking about the fear so much that you could become afraid to be in crowds. Afraid to go back to

## Chapter 4 - How to Break the Barrier

the place where the robbery occurred. This one incident could change how you approach life going forward. Years ago, I was working as a bank teller for a few months. I was asked to come to work on my day off to cover for a co-worker. That day, I was stationed closest to the door and furthest from everyone. A man came into our bank. He was wearing sunglasses and a baseball cap and appeared to be hearing impaired. He could not speak, so he was writing down questions about setting up an account with my manager, then he left the bank.

About thirty minutes later, I saw the same man standing in line, waiting for a teller. I noticed he was letting people go ahead of him. Then I realized that he was waiting for me. He had a brown paper bag in his hand. He walked up to the counter and handed me a note. The note said he had a gun and that he wanted me to put all the money in my drawer in his bag. He warned me to not use any dyes or alarms because he had someone outside who would hurt everyone if I didn't do what he said. Remain calm and do what he said, and no one would get hurt. He then pulled out the gun from the bag and set in on the counter to show me he wasn't bluffing.

At that moment, I went into survival mode. It was like everything around me stopped, and the only thing in that moment that was real was him and me. I pulled the silent alarm even though I was scared to do it because he had said, no alarms. I did what he said and put the money in the bag. I asked him if he wanted my coins, too, and then he turned around, and headed out the door. I turned to my co-worker, who was two stations down and told him I was just robbed. He asked me, "What did you just say?" Then I found my voice, and yelled to my manager, "I was just robbed."

They closed all the doors and called the police. The FBI came and interrogated me. It felt like they were trying to make me feel like I had done something wrong. I didn't cry until after everything was over because I was in shock. After a while, I went to work for another bank. A few months after being there, I was working the front counter, and a man with sunglasses and a baseball cap came up to my station. I froze. I couldn't move. The fear of what had happened to me before was there all over again. I was reliving that moment and feeling all the fear I had experienced. The man became angry because he didn't understand why I was acting the way I was. A co-worker had to do the transaction because I had to walk away and compose myself.

My grief counselor told me I experienced post-traumatic stress. I usually worked the drive-through counter, but after the incident, I asked to not work at the front counter anymore and to work the drive-through only. I chose to not let the incident keep me from doing my job, but I had to change how I work to feel secure. I now understand how people feel when they are in survival mode and why they will do whatever is necessary to keep themselves and others safe.

Being the victim in a situation I had no control over was a real eye-opener for me. I could have chosen to hide in fear, or I could have become a recluse, too afraid to leave my house. I could have chosen to stop working at the bank. I could have chosen to believe that the world is a bad place, and I'm a victim of this world. I went to counseling, which helped me work through my fear. I decided to not dwell on it and move on. I am thankful that it wasn't a lot worse than it could have been, thankful that no one was physically injured. It taught me to have more compassion for people who are the victims of crimes and circumstances for those that have PTSD. My heart goes out to them. Many people have had far worse experiences than me, such as the men and women in our military. I cannot even begin to comprehend what they have gone through.

## Chapter 4 - How to Break the Barrier

A family member of mine has served in the military for half of their lifetime and has been in Afghanistan and Iraq. I have seen firsthand the effects of PTSD and do not discount how serious it is.

How can one possibly change beliefs that don't serve them? Try to start changing beliefs about what happened. Start asking questions or saying statements that empower you instead of causing fear and making you stay in a victim mindset. Statements like 'I want to make this incident something that makes me stronger.' Then you can start thinking of ways to keep getting better like, 'Maybe I can start a support group for victims' or 'I should take a self-defense class that makes me feel less venerable and more powerful again.'

Yes, the incident happened, and at the time it was scary, but you are NOT living it right now. Change life circumstances if you don't feel safe. Take something positive from the experience, something that can help you grow instead of possibly becoming a long-term victim. Embrace the difficult experiences and learn from them. Celebrate hard times and know they are there to teach us lessons.

If you go through something traumatic and you just can't overcome it, find resources like counseling, reaching out to other people to help you through it. I think counseling is a great way to help change our beliefs. Someone outside of the situation can have a different perspective and can allow you to look at the situation in a better light. When things seem to be more than you can handle, "Let go, let God."

## Chapter 5
## Forgiveness

*Most of us need time to work through pain and loss. We can find all manner of reasons for postponing forgiveness. One of these reasons is waiting for the wrongdoers to repent before we forgive them. Yet such a delay causes us to forfeit the peace and happiness that could be ours.*

*-James E. Fost*

Forgiving people in our past can be a very difficult thing. Trust me, I know from experience. I love my father; I forgave him years ago. But that wasn't always the case in our relationship. I had a difficult childhood. I was a sickly child from the start. I suffered from allergies, and *many* foods were off-limits. I'm allergic to dust, grass, weeds, and mold. Allergic to all animals with fur. I would get eczema rashes all over my body. As a child, my mom would give me tar baths. Then she would grease me down with steroid creams, wrap me in saran wrap, and put socks on my hands hoping that my skin would heal and I wouldn't scratch all night. I also had asthma, so breathing could be a problem at times.

My dad worked in construction, so we moved around a lot. I went to six different elementary schools. Making friends was hard for me, and it felt like every time I made a friend, we would have to move again. After a while, it hurt too much to make friends just to turn around and lose them. As a result, I usually was alone and kept to myself on the playground. I was usually the smallest child in my class, and because I kept to myself, I got picked on a lot by the other kids.

Thank God I had my sister there with me. She is three years younger than I am, and we did everything together. I could be a mean big sister at times, but we usually had fun and got along well. One thing my Dad really didn't like was to be woken up, usually because he was hungover. It made him so angry! I remember one time my sister was jumping on her bed early in the morning. I told her to stop, or she would wake Dad up, but she didn't listen. He woke up. Angry and hungover. He came in with a belt and whipped us, covering us in black and blue bruises across our legs, back, and butt.

That night my mom gave us our baths, and she was horrified at the sight. She brought him in and showed him the bruises, and she said, "You better not ever hurt my babies again, or I will leave you." My dad replied, "Fine, if they are your babies, then you can take care of them." He never hit us again, but when we misbehaved - as all children do - he would tell our mother that if she would have let him raise us his way, we would be better children.

He always made it seem like it was her fault that we were misbehaving. This made me feel bad for my mother. More than once, I remember him saying that he never wanted children. If he didn't have us around, he could have afforded nicer things. You should never tell a child they are unwanted, hearing that can really hurt the self-esteem. My dad didn't tell me he loved me until I was around eighteen years old. He never showed me

## Chapter 5 - Forgiveness

affection growing up. I remember trying to hug him when I was a little girl, but he just pushed me away. Told me to leave him alone. That he was busy watching television.

Being a little girl who wanted her Daddy's love and attention was not an easy thing to overcome. I became angry at my father because I felt like he didn't love me. It is awful to not have a parent be there for you when you need them. This gave me a lot of self-esteem issues. I felt like there was something wrong with me – that I wasn't good enough for my Daddy to love me. I wasn't even sure if I loved him. But there is one thing I did know – my mom loved me.

I had struggled with "daddy issues" for part of my life, and I spent a lot of time in counseling trying to move past them. My romantic relationships with men had been unhealthy. I didn't want to have kids because I was worried that I would pass down my father's parenting style. I didn't want to be anything like my Dad with my children. Luckily, over time, I came to realize that I don't have to be like him. I can break the chain and be a loving parent instead.

I can see now how my father didn't have it easy, either. His mother had been physically abusive to him. His father left him when he was a small child because he didn't want kids. Now that I am an adult and a parent, I see from a different set of eyes than the ones I had as a child.

I could have stayed a victim and said it was my Dad's fault that my marriages didn't work, but now I understand that my Dad was only doing what he thought was right at the time. My Dad only knew what he had learned from his childhood. My Mom and Dad split up after thirty-one years of marriage. He was heartbroken, it made him decide he wanted to have a better relationship with his daughters.

Every Sunday morning, he would come by my place with coffee and doughnuts, and we would sit and visit. We talked about things in the past and what was happening at the time. I got to know my Dad as an adult and learn things I never knew about him.

I grew to love my dad very much and forgave him. My dad ended up getting leukemia, and though he fought it well, we knew it was killing him. His second wife was an RN and was able to give him the extra care he needed. He was in and out of the hospital often. Needless to say, I was worried about him.

I was living in Colorado at the time, and he was living in Arizona. I was planning on going out to Arizona after a trip to Las Vegas for a stock trading class and to do an interview for this book.

He called me from the hospital and asked when he would see me. I told him I would be there on October 27. Every day, we would talk, and he would ask me, "What day are you coming here?" I would tell him on October 27.

On October 27, 2014, I was with him in his room at home. With his wife and the hospice nurse beside me, he took his last breath and transitioned from his body. I held onto him, and I cried. Even now, I can still feel the pain of the loss I felt in that moment, as tears roll down my face. I miss him every day, I wish we could talk again. I'm so glad I was able to truly forgive my Dad and have a good relationship with him before he passed.

Forgiveness is for the forgiver – not for the other person. We need to forgive those who have hurt us in the past. Many people feel like 'there is no way I can ever forgive them for what they did to me!' but remember, *forgiveness is not for them but rather for you.*

Any anger and hatred that you carry around all day and that keeps you awake at night is causing stress in your body and mind. The only one who is being hurt by this anger and hate is you. A lot of times the person we are angry at doesn't even know that we

## Chapter 5 - Forgiveness

are angry at them. And even if they do, they may just not care the same way you do. You may be beside yourself while they go on living their life.

We forgive to let go of the pain and anger and stress we feel. The person we are angry at can't feel any of the feelings we are feeling now. Don't create suffering for yourself by holding on to these feelings. You may not forget what they did or the hurt it caused you, but we all need to find peace for ourselves, so we can have a better life. You don't even have to tell the person that you forgive them if you don't want to. You always have the choice if you want to or not.

The other important factor is we must forgive ourselves. We tend to beat ourselves, up more than anyone else ever could. Forgiving ourselves can be so healing! If you feel like you can't forgive another person or yourself right now, then try giving it to God, Jesus, Allah, Buddha, or whichever entity you believe in. I want to remind you, let the pain go, and I'll say it again, "Let go, Let God."

When we have an experience with someone that really upset us, it was upsetting in the moment. The more we tell the story over and over in our heads or to others, the more it grows. It becomes a bigger deal. You may find more emotions are there, it makes the whole situation feel bigger than it was, to begin with. We need to stop telling ourselves upsetting stories, over and over like a broken record in our head. We need to accept what happened and move on.

So how do we move on? First, acknowledge that being angry about the past is only making you the victim here. Being the victim means you are letting what they did control you - instead of stepping up and taking control of your life from a place of non-victimhood. Second, look at the part you played in the situation and take responsibility for what you may have done. Third, look at their situation and maybe see why they did what they did. Ask yourself what you may have done if you were in their shoes. Lastly, think about how the situation may have made you grow or become stronger because of experiencing it.

Life is too short to be angry over something from the past that you can't change. It only poisons us. I was angry for years at my ex-husband for what he did to me and to my son, but now I feel nothing toward my ex-husband. I can't change what he did, and by being angry, it only hurts me. Forgiveness sets us free! If you can come from a place of true forgiveness for yourself and those who do you wrong - you will be set free.

## Chapter 6
## Why

*And once the storm is over you won't remember how you made it through, how you managed to survive. You won't even be sure, in fact, whether the storm is really over. But one thing is certain. When you come out of the storm, you won't be the same person who walked in. That's what the storm is all about.*
  *~ Haruki Murakami, Kafka on the shore*

We all ask the question, why? Why did this happen to me? There are times in our lives when the wind gets knocked out of our sails. When we get blindsided and say, 'I never saw that coming.' Times when we may fall to our knees in sorrow – asking the question, why?

I will never forget the night I got the phone call around 2:00 in the morning. I didn't recognize the number, but I knew it was a call from Idaho. My oldest son lives in Idaho, so I answered it. It was my son's mother-in-law, and my heart dropped when she told me who she was and why she was calling. She told me that my only grandchild died. My son and daughter-in-law were at the hospital.

They had checked on the baby and found he wasn't breathing. Nothing they did helped, they couldn't get him to breathe. The doctors pronounced the cause of death to be SIDS, which is sudden infant death syndrome.

I cried non-stop for twenty-four hours. The pain I felt was unbearable, and the emptiness of never getting to see my grandson grow up filled my soul. I cried for me, I cried for my son and my daughter-in-law. I cried for my grandson, whose little life was cut short at 5 months. When I think about it, I still cry. Why? Why did this have to happen?

We all experience different tragedies in our lives that don't seem fair. The only choice we have is to move on, no matter how hard it feels or how much it hurts. Moving on is not always the easier route – sometimes it seems easier to fall back into victim mode and not let go. But, I have found that not letting go is actually harder on us and can hurt us more in the long run.

Now, when I say moving on or letting go, I'm not suggesting that you are not supposed to stop mourning your losses or forget the people or things we have lost that were dear to us. But you must stop second-guessing why it happened or why it happened the way it did. You could go crazy thinking about the reasons why. You need to stop asking why stop possibly beating yourself up. Stop second guessing what else could have been done or questioning why God had to do this because the truth is you may never know why. The reality is we rarely get to know why.

Maybe this challenging circumstance that is making you ask WHY may help you choose a different path on your journey. Maybe you experienced a loss so you could help someone else with their loss. Don't let this questioning consume your heart and soul until there is nothing.

## Chapter 6 - WHY?

After losing my grandson, I had to stop asking why so that I wouldn't turn into the empty shell of what I felt or let bitterness and anger replace my joy. Joy and peace are what we should strive for. If you are stuck asking why right now, be strong my friend, and look for love, and peace to fill your heart!

# A New and Powerful You

## Chapter 7
## Grief

*When you lose something in your life, stop thinking it's a loss for you... it is a gift you have been given so you can get on the right path to where you are meant to go, not to where you think you should have gone.*

*~Suze Orman*

Feelings of grief can paralyze us and keep us stuck. It can keep us from growing to our full potential. It can leave us angry. It can leave us hurting for a long time. It is important that you are working through the emotions surrounding your grief. Sometimes you may not even know that you are grieving over something. You know you have strong feelings surrounding a loss but may not know that grief is what is causing these feelings.

My fiancé, JC, and I had been fighting because he had gone over to the casinos and had not come home the night before. The night before his murder, he came to my door. I had just started working a new job. After a long day, I came home late, and I was exhausted. He told me that he wanted to talk about the reasons he was not home and had some good news, but I was very tired.

I replied that we could talk the next day instead. He asked if he could at least see his daughter while he was there. I told him no, she was sleeping, maybe tomorrow. His turned to leave, and his last words to me were, "I want you to know that no matter what happens, I will always love you."

It turned out there was no tomorrow for us. It was the third day of my new job. My manager wanted to talk to me, and my first thought to myself were that I was going to be fired. I went into the room where the manager was. Some of my friends were there, which was confusing. They told me they wanted to be the first ones to tell me the news that JC was dead, he was murdered.

I collapsed to the floor instantly and let out a cry of intense grief as my heart broke. There would never be another tomorrow with him – never again. I would never hold him again. I could never see his face again. His daughter would never know her dad. It was a moment that changed me, and I have never been the same person since. His death was very devastating for me. I loved him with all my heart like no other.

I spent five years in grief counseling, and it took me three years to come to a point of acceptance of his death. I would spend hours at his grave site listening to "our" songs. I cried till I could cry no more.

The pain was so intense, but I realized the pain was more than just his death. It was also compounded by the grief that I had when I lost my child to John. The hurt was overwhelming.

Grief can tear us apart. We all experience loss in our life. Loss could mean losing a loved one, a special relationship, or a cherished pet. It could mean losing a job or your health, there are so many losses we can experience as we go through life. The bad part about grief is that we can carry it around for a lifetime, and it can affect us in ways that we may not see. I would like to say that I have worked through all the pain from the losses in my life – but I have not. I still have wounds that need to heal. All I can

## Chapter 7 - Grief

do is continue to work through them and remind myself that life is about finding our way. I still grieve over the loss of my hair and wish I had it back.

When we first experience a major loss, we go into a state of shock. It is a coping mechanism for our brains to reach for denial first. We may feel anger, guilt, or helplessness set in. If you are a religious person, you may or may not become angry with God during this time or find some peace by practicing your religion. We may or may not question ourselves about what we could have done differently. We may or may not go through a stage of depression where we experience extreme sadness, feeling overwhelmed, or a loneliness that leaves us with not wanting to sleep or eat. You may need to talk about it, or you may want to hold your thoughts and feelings in. We handle our losses differently.

Healing from grief is not always easy - but it is important. My experience is the pain from grief is like no other pain. There is nothing that can subdue or take away that pain except for time. The waves of pain we can feel could be unbearable at times while your heart is breaking, and everything hurts. I personally found that sometimes I felt very alone. I felt like there was no one around who could imagine how deep the pain is. But I have learned that *the waves of pain do become less painful over time.*

There are many things you can do to lessen your grief. Some good options include reading books on grieving, seeing a grief counselor. Reaching out to the people around you who could help you from their experiences. Talking to the right person during this time can help you take steps to move beyond feeling stuck. I worked with a grief counselor for a few years after the death of my fiancé.

Through counseling, I found layers of other emotional issues that had only intensified the grief. Sometimes grief unburies the emotions that we have tried to push down or avoid. This can make it feel like you are dealing with everything all at once because the grief can intensify your emotions. One thing that was important for my healing was to talk to others who had also experienced a loss. There are many support groups out there and lots of people who are willing to listen and help. There are others going through something similar. At a grief support program, I had checked into, a gentleman shared with the group that he had been deployed, and while he was away, someone broke into his home and raped and murdered his wife. I couldn't even imagine his pain or all the other emotions that he must have had after something so horrifying happened. Yet he inspired and helped me because he was willing to reach out to others and give them support.

Helpful Habits to practice when you are experiencing grief:
- Give yourself time. Know that grieving is a process
- Take care of yourself. Make sure you eat healthy and regularly, even when you don't feel like it. Get enough sleep. Take time to exercise
- Do activities and hobbies that make you happy
- Talk to others. Avoid isolating yourself from friends and family
- Join a support group, remember you never need to be alone in your grief

Grief is a part of life. The price of loving or caring about something and losing it - is grief - it is a two-edged sword. The price of love can be grief, but to love is such a blessing and so beautiful.

## Chapter 8
## Dark Night of the Soul

*The situations that will stretch your faith most will be those times when life falls apart and God is nowhere to be found. This happened to Job.*
— Rick Warren

What is the dark night of the soul? The term usually describes a spiritual crisis in the journey of moving toward a union with God. For me, it was finding God but not the God I knew before.

I would like to share my experience of the dark night of the soul with you. Please know, this is my own experience, and I am not trying to influence anyone's religious beliefs. I would like to relay my own beliefs and experiences at the time and ask for you to read without judgment.

I don't believe that everyone experiences a dark night of the soul. At first, I thought it was a bad experience to have. And it is, especially while you are going through it. But as I have grown in my spirituality, I now choose to see it as another stepping stone on my journey to become who I am today. I believe these dark times are truly a blessing once you reach the end of the journey.

I once went through the dark night of the soul for 8 long years. I felt completely lost. Everything I had believed in up until this time was now gone. I was in deep depression. I felt like I had no purpose and that God had forsaken me. Instead of having him by my side as he was when I grew up, I was left to face my pain alone. No one around me seemed to understand this.

It all started with the tragic death of my fiancé, the father of my beautiful 15-month-old daughter at the time. The very night I learned of his death, I went to seek support at the church. The people there told me that since he had not possibly been "saved," he probably went straight to hell. I tried to find consolation in the church, but I felt instead that people in my church ridiculed me for my love for a man who was not a member of the church. I was so devastated by this response that everything I had ever believed in about God came tumbling down around me. How could a loving god and father send his child to hell for not being "perfect?"

God had been my best friend growing up. I would talk to him about everything, just like I would a best friend. I would ask Jesus to wrap me in his arms at night if I was scared, and the fear would go away. But now it seemed like things had changed, and God had left. I told God I was walking away if it meant someone good whom I loved was in hell. From that night on, it seemed as if I was praying in vain. I no longer felt his presence as I once did.

When I was growing up, God was always an important part of my life. I prayed every night. I went to Sunday school and church camp in the summers. I attended different affiliations of the Christian church.

## Chapter 8 - Dark Night of the Soul

    I immersed myself into the church looking for answers to the one question I had that bothered me the most. If God is our Father, why would a loving father send his beloved children to hell, the worst place imaginable?

    God had been very important to me for as long as I could remember. This was the beginning of the journey of my dark night of the soul. Feeling so differently about God and not knowing how to change it made this a very challenging time for me. I knew I could never go back to the relationship I had with God before, but I knew I wanted a relationship with God. I had a big empty void inside of me without the closeness to God that I had always known.

    I knew I could not go back to the same church or what I believed before. I would ask people where I might go next on my spiritual journey. They would tell me that God was in my heart, always with me, had never left me. I wondered, if he was in heaven, how could he also be there in my heart? I had been looking at God as someone with a long white beard on a throne in heaven. I imagined that when you die, you go to heaven, and this white-bearded man looks in his book of life. If your name is there, then you get to live happily ever after. I also believed hell was only for the bad people. The kind who never ask for forgiveness for doing bad things. This always made me think. If God is a loving father, why would he send his child to hell because no child is perfect? As a parent myself, I know I would forgive and love my child no matter what they did.

    So I stumbled around for 8 years in this time of depression without God. It also turned out to be a time of change in my life. Multiple people in my life recommended a certain church to me and told me that that church might be what I was looking for. I didn't feel ready to try another church, but I decided I would try it anyway since so many people had said it was "different," and it would help me find what I was seeking. After my first experience at this church. I was intrigued, and I went a few more times. They had a 6-week class on religious abuse. The class was for those who had felt in the name of religion or God some form of abuse, whether it be emotional or physical. I went to the class, and I learned that there were other people there, experiencing a dark night of the soul too. It was spiritually healing for me, and after 8 years, I had finally found a church I could call home.

My spiritual healing did not happen overnight. It took many years since my spirit was hurt and broken. It can take a lot of faith and searching within yourself in order to find God. I took other classes that the church offered to deepen my understanding and faith. I learned the lesson that others had tried to tell me that God was in my heart the whole time. I learned that we are children of God, and each of us are connected to God. There is no separation as he lives and expresses through us.

God is so much more to me now, more than a man sitting on a throne in heaven. I have found so much peace and joy with the spiritual part of my life. I love the spiritual aspects of life more than I ever did when I was young or before my dark night of the soul journey.

## Chapter 9
## Spirituality

*I believe deeply that we must find, all of us together, a new spirituality. This new concept ought to be elaborated alongside the religions in such a way that all people of good will could adhere to it.*

*- The Dalai Lama*

What is the thing called spirituality? It is a word that may have a different meaning to many different people. People can define spirituality differently and has different ideas about it. I have found on my journey that almost all religions have something in common, and that is, there is a higher power, and we need to love one another as we love ourselves.

I believe spirituality is important because it gives us connection to a source greater than ourselves. I believe this is important for many reasons. Believing there is a greater source can give us something to hold onto when we feel hopeless, or in despair or lonely. Without it, I feel like I have no compass to guide me through my life. When times get tough, I have God to lean on and help me get through the tough times more easily than if I thought I was alone.

As I have grown on my spiritual path, I have come to believe that there is no separation of our spirits from that of God's and that we are all children of God. Two verses from the bible that inspire me are, "Do you not know that you are the temple of God and that the Spirit of God dwells in you?" (1 Cor. 3:16, Lamas Version) and "For I am convinced that neither death nor life, neither angels nor demons, neither the present nor the future, nor any powers, neither height nor depth, nor anything else in all creation, will be able to separate us from the love of God that is in Christ Jesus our Lord."(Romans 8:38-39)

With access to this source or God, we can create anything we want. We are pure energy, so we are all connected through the energy we share. We are one with the creator, and we can co-create anything we want in our lives. We can co-create with the creator, and when we realize this, it opens a whole new world for us. When we try to create without love, we create things we don't want in our lives. God is love, and we need to create from a place of love in order to have what we truly need. We are body and spirit. If we connect with our spirit, we can open so many doors.

We are so much more than our physical bodies. We are connected to the divine, we are one with the divine, and we are connected to all things in creation.

As Albert Einstein said, "Everything is energy, and that's all there is to it. Match the frequency of the reality you want, and you cannot help but get that reality. It can be no other way. This is not philosophy. This is physics."

## Chapter 9 - Spirituality

Ernest Holmes, the founder of The Church of Religious Science, said,

*If we believe that the Father is within us, and if we believe that all things are possible with God, then we should no longer deny that God knows what to do with His own creation, and we should include ourselves in that creation.*

I learned a lot from the Mile Hi Church in Denver. It brought me out of my dark night of the soul journey. It gave me a new perspective of God and religion. I became a happier person. I'm excited to have an interview with Dr. Roger Teel in the next chapter. He is the senior minister of Mile Hi Church.

# Chapter 10
## An Interview with Dr. Roger on Spirituality

*We can no more do without spirituality than we can do without food, shelter, or clothing.*
*~Ernest Holmes*

I would like to dedicate this chapter to a man who is well respected and loved by thousands of people in the Denver community. I had the pleasure to interview him for this book. I met Dr. Roger at Mile Hi Church, when he was the senior minister. However, he has recently retired.

On March 14, 1960, Mile Hi Church was officially recognized as an affiliated church with the Church of Religious Science. The Church of Religious Science was founded by a man named Ernest Holmes.

I interviewed Dr. Roger Teel to get his ideas and views on spirituality. I find them very enlightening, and I hope you do too. Dr. Roger Teel has been a minister for 40 years in the teachings of

Science of Mind, also referred to as Religious Science. He started his spiritual journey with a mystical experience as a six-year-old child, which led him on his spiritual journey. He has written a book called "This Life is Joy: Discovering the Spiritual Laws to Live More Powerfully, Lovingly, and Happily." Dr. Roger is a global spiritual leader and co-founder of the Association for Global New Thought (AGNT), an organization dedicated to "consciously bringing forth the evolving human and an awakened world through the practice of universal spiritual principles and the energy of unconditional love." He is also one of the most beautiful souls I have ever met.

My first question for Dr. Roger was, 'what daily practices would he recommend for a more peaceful and joyful life?' His advice is;

> *Without a doubt, meditation and prayer are two things to practice daily. Meditation is a deep centering, and it's attuning to the presence of the Spirit, which is everywhere present. The mind which can only comprehend a small amount of life will be present and available to the larger whole. That can only be found in the stillness. It is not a mental activity; it is stilling the mind and attuning into the Great Spirit. Our society today is so busy with doing and resisting the idea of slowing down and being still. Affirmative prayer is what we teach here at Mile Hi Church. Affirmative prayer is building that deep silent knowingness into conscious spiritual awareness and directing it towards manifestation. With the understanding that we are all designed to be conscious co-creators with God, and that we create in the same way God creates, from the invisible to the visible, from the idea to the form. As we form clear concepts and new ideas empowered by faith, then they can take form in our lives. I would also add spiritual study and spiritual fellowship. I think they are important as well.*

## Chapter 10 - An interview with Dr. Roger on Spirituality

I asked Dr. Roger what some of his favorite affirmations are and his response was;

*I like the one that Dr. Holmes said, "there is a powerful good in the universe greater than I am and I can use it" and also "God is always conspiring for my highest and best" it helps remind myself that there is a power working to support me. And some simple affirmations, "I am love, I am peace, and I am joy." The purpose of affirmations is to activate a higher awareness within us. Not to just be saying things but to really create the feeling. We do these affirmations to lift our consciousness to a higher level.*

To sum up, what I believe Dr. Roger is saying is that by doing daily affirmations with feeling, not just saying them can produce better results. And because we are co-creators with God, we can create in the same way God creates. Meditation is important because it gives us a place of stillness so that God, spirit, or source can connect or speak to us. My next question for Dr. Roger was, 'We all face challenges in our lives-what advice can you give someone who is facing a challenge?'

*When we are in a challenge, we need to look at our viewpoint. When an obstacle or problem comes along, we usually judge it initially and say it is negative or call it a problem and make it big and large. Our viewpoint is very important. We need to change our position regarding the challenge. Most people in a challenge position themselves as victims or products of the challenge rather than as co-creators with God. We must reclaim our sense of being co-creators, that is the first thing. Then we need to look at our intentions when problems come along, let the problem teach us, and grow from it. We need to summon a deeper belief in ourselves; realize that we may be having a problem, but we are not the problem. Many let problems dominate everything about them, and then like quicksand, let it pull them under. It's one thing to have a problem, but we need to remember who we really are. We are spiritual beings - we are magnificent and joyful beings. Part of a challenge is to reposition ourselves in terms of the truth as beings, we need to reclaim that truth and stand in that truth so we can dream.*

*It is very important to remember that there is a divine mind counterpart for every problem or challenge. We may be facing a problem and may not know the solution, but God knows. There is an answer to this problem waiting to revel itself. We need to keep our selves open - so the reveling of the answer can come through us and guide us. Sometimes problems have a way of being so intimidating that we forget there is a larger life. There is a solution already known, ready in the mind of God, ready to come forth. It is about changing our viewpoint, reclaiming the truth about ourselves, and remembering that we can dream. We need to stand in our faith and remember that we are children of God.*

*Remember that we are given these spiritual resources to walk through these dark nights and that we are not alone, we are supported. We need to get back to the truth of who we really are. Remember that you are part of something greater, that's not only loving you now and supporting you, but it already knows the higher answer to this problem. Keep your awareness and hearts open. That is the way we spiritually walk through a challenge.*

# Chapter 10 - An interview with Dr. Roger on Spirituality

To sum it up, Dr. Roger is saying that we can make the problem bigger and need to remember that God knows the solution. By keeping your faith and heart open, you can find the solution. Remember that we are children of God.

I asked Roger if he could explain what he meant by co-create with God. His answer;

*We are partners with God in manifesting a higher good for our lives, the divine already holds all possibilities for us. Jesus said, "Before I even ask it, it is already given." As an individual, we have a job assignment in that we must believe it. We must be an open channel for it; otherwise, all that is God is blocked from expressing in your life. The divine has already created the potential for every good thing for you. We co-create that good by remembering and believing in what Jesus said and being open to it. Then the already created answer and or already created opportunity or healing or wholeness can come through you. Remember our good in life does not come to us, we may think it does, but it comes through us. It comes through our believing, our consciousness, through our alignment with Spirit.*

To sum up what Dr. Roger is saying, things in life come through us by our beliefs, faith, and knowing that we co-create with God.

I asked Dr. Roger, 'Can you explain how there is no separation from God and how we are all connected?' His answer was;

*I don't know if I can explain it, but that is the truth because that is the grace of how God set things up. If you really think about it, there is only one ultimate life force. One life presence, everything that it creates must be created within it and of it. Because ultimately all there is, is that life, so it has nothing to create anything out of by itself. And its own ideas are the seed of life in everything, so the Divine Mind has all possibilities… so let there be, and it was, and it is good.*

*So that is the difference in our teachings, we do not believe there are competing and warring forces in this universe that it's good and evil or a competing God and Satan. We believe that evil is the lower consciousness in humankind allowed to influence human choices. God is love, and out of that love, God has imparted Gods own spirit into creation ascended into creation. And yet there is no out there - because that creates duality as well - so all there is - is God. Everything must be created of that divine spirit, divine light, and must live within it too. This is the shift in world view that this teaching offers people.*

*It is consistent with Quantum Science that everything is part of a unified field of pure potential. Out of this field - this invisible field of potential - the visible or the material comes forth. This is not primarily a material universe - we may think it is. But we do deal with this material world of ours, but the universe is a world of intelligence and is a potential life force waiting to come forth as expression. So as co-creators, we are a channel for which life force can move into form. We participate by shaping our own ideas and our own possibilities and bringing forth our own uniqueness to the world, that's the way Spirit becomes more fluent.*

*Oneness - there is no spot where God is not. Even in a situation where it seems like there is a total breakdown or total absence of an answer or a darkness of some kind. We suggest that is only what it appears to be, but the higher truth is right in the*

## Chapter 10 - An interview with Dr. Roger on Spirituality

*midst of it. In the midst of the darkness, the light is prepared to shine. It is calling on us to light that candle and calling on us to bring that light forth.*

To sum up what Dr. Roger is saying, there is only one life force, there is no spot that God is not. That God expresses himself through us, and he can take form through us by our ideas and uniqueness.

I then asked Dr. Rodger, 'Prayer can be very powerful, can you tell me of an experience that showed the power of prayer working in your life?'

*There are so many times that come to mind; but there was a time when we were in a building campaign, and we wanted to build a new sanctuary. We had an architect that had worked on several designs, and during that time, steel and concrete prices were going out the roof - this was around 2006-2007. The design didn't seem right, so I took it to prayer. I said, alright, Infinite Mind, I know there is a right idea for this church. I know there is a design that will serve in wonderful ways that are cost efficient. I affirm that idea exists, I know that it exists. I know that it is being revealed to me or too someone in the right time and right moment. I accept this and, I direct this to be done through the law - so it is.*

*Then I went about my business. A couple days later, I was cleaning out some office drawers. I came across an old brochure that was given to me many years ago. It was about a company that builds domes in a new and different way. I thought I would call the company and see if they were still building domes. I called them, and they were still doing domes and building them in a lot of places. They showed us what could be done. That is what we did—it sits out there now. By the way, you could say it was by accident but no. I don't clean out my drawers very often – so it was no accident. For some reason, I felt the need to clean out my drawers, and then I stumbled onto the brochure – it was not a coincidence. I have prayed for so many people in this church. I have seen physical healings. I've seen people lifted out of depression; I have seen it all.*

I asked Dr. Rodger, 'I know humor can be some of the best medicine-would you mind sharing a humorous experience you have had in your spiritual journey?'

*I have had a bunch of those. What came to my mind first, when I read the question was when I was a minister working with my beloved mentor Fred Vogt. I was still a little insecure. I had only been in the ministry maybe four or five years, and the secretary sent a call to me. I picked up the phone, and this gentleman started launching about a terrible sermon last Sunday. I had been the one to give the talk that Sunday, he was saying it had not been well organized and was superficial. I started to feel my anger rising and thinking you don't know what it takes to write a sermon - you probably have never written a sermon in your life. You're criticizing me and being cruel and getting me all upset. Then he said, "so I got up and left that church and came over here and listened to you, and it made all the difference in the world." It was such a lesson to look at my own insecurities and my own defensiveness. The guy's intention was to compliment me, and I had shifted into thinking the guy was criticizing me. I had to laugh at myself. One thing about our teaching of Science of Mind - it is meant to be joyous. Those that have made spirituality fearful and guilt ridden and somber have done a disservice to spirituality.*

## Chapter 10 - An interview with Dr. Roger on Spirituality

*I have had the privilege of being around some very spiritual people. I have been with his Holiness the Dalai Lama three times. One of those times, I had lunch with him at a conference I co-facilitated in Italy. This man is carrying the weight of genocide, which is happening in his homeland of Tibet, seeing the destruction of his culture and sacred writings. Yet, he is still laughing and has joy because he knows there is a larger truth. He is not a superficial person to any degree, but he is not letting his soul get captured by what is going on. He knows there is a higher reality going on. Our founder Dr. Holmes said there should be a sense of joy in our work. The name of my book is "This Life is Joy." There is a deeper joy within us, there is a spirit in us that doesn't toil or strain, it is the joy of God.*

I then asked Dr. Rodger, 'What spiritual and healing experiences could you share with us?' Dr. Rodger said;

*I think it is important to say there is nothing too great for God! I've seen people just given weeks to live, and they had total remission. I think it is also important to recognize that there are many forms of healing. I have seen times in my life when something totally broke down and at the time thought it to be awful, but proved to be one of the best things in my life. I've seen individuals leave their bodies and pass on. Some people think it is terrible it happened; but it is not, we are spiritual beings, we are immortal - we are part of life itself. This body is just a physical garment-it is not who we really are. When we lay it aside, there is no injury to the soul - it goes on to grow and expand. Even when the individual leaves the body or a loved one leaves the body, we do our natural grieving - we grieve because we have loved. And yet we can also know that all things work together for good. That is an affirmation I want to leave with you, "that all things work together for good." We are wonderful beings and need to remember who we really are. Believe beautiful things about ourselves. Before things can change, we must change within first, then things outside of us can change. Life is meant to be good.*

I'm so thankful that I was able to interview Dr. Rodger as he is now retired. I hope you enjoyed reading this chapter as much as I enjoyed spending the time speaking with him and sharing his wisdom.

# Chapter 11
## My Journey Back Home

*We can never obtain peace in the outer world
until we make peace with ourselves.
~ The Dalai Lama*

I wanted to share this story with hopes that it may give you some insight on my life when I was going through the beginnings of my Dark Night of the Soul journey. Even though I felt so distant from God during that time, he was always there watching over me - protecting me and my children.

It had been almost a year since the murder of my fiancé. It was January, and I was living in Arizona. I was a single mom. My daughter was two years old, my son from my first marriage was 9 years old, and my middle son was somewhere in Colorado with John. I had been going to grief counseling, but I felt the urge to go back home to the Denver area where I had family. I also hoped that maybe, John would let me see my son. I wanted to go back to the familiar places where I had grown up. I thought maybe a change from everything that reminded me of JC would be healing. And it was. The trip was about 850 miles. I bought my deceased fiancés' 1972 Cadillac from his parents. I rented the biggest U-Haul trailer I could pull with the car. I loaded it up with everything that I owned. I said my goodbyes to the friends I had made in Arizona and headed out of town. It was starting to get dark, and I was coming upon a mountain pass west of Flagstaff that was requiring chains. I pulled over to the side of the road, and a nice trucker put the chains on for me. The snow was starting to come down fast and hard as the darkness was enfolding us. I was scared and had never felt so alone as I did in that moment. I asked God to send the angels down to protect me and my children.

I looked over the hood of the car and saw a shimmering light on each corner of the hood. Maybe it was the reflection of the headlights off the snow, but in my mind, I knew immediately it was the angels! They were there to protect and guide us. I kept my eyes on the road as we went slow and steady up the steep mountain pass. It seemed we were the only car on the road; they must have closed the highway. No other headlights or cars were to be seen, except the ones banked in the ditches that we saw as we drove past. It seemed like forever before we got to the top of the pass. I took the first exit I came to and looked for a motel. I found a motel and got the last available room.

The next morning, we got up and continued our journey to Flagstaff. The only problem was that I needed to get the chains off my tires. I didn't have the strength to unhook them myself. We went five miles an hour on the highway. One of the chains had come loose, but I couldn't get it off. I finally found a gas station who would remove them, but they wanted $50 to take my chains off. I had only a small amount of cash – I decided not to spend it there. I needed what little money I had for gas and food. Instead, I got back on the highway. It was slow-moving, and we were not even halfway to Denver.

## Chapter 11 - My Journey Back Home

I came upon another gas station, and they agreed to take the chains off for free. All I could think was, "thank you, God!" After they got the chains off, the attendant, said "You were pretty lucky! The chains were wrapped around your brake line-it could have broken. You would have been without brakes. Someone is definitely watching over you! You do need to get shocks because the weight of the U-Haul could break your brake lines. We don't install shocks here; but about three miles down the road, there is a garage that will."

When I got there, they said they could put shocks on, but it would cost $200. That was all the money I had left. I had no idea what I was I going to do. I told the man at the garage I couldn't afford to fix the car even though I desperately needed to. He asked me if I could get the money from my husband or someone else. I said I didn't have a husband. After I said that, he took a good look at my situation. He saw a single woman with two little children, who was pulling behind her car a U-Haul with all her worldly belongings, and he took pity on me. My sad predicament must have touched his heart because he said, "Okay, this is what I can do. I can put in spacers that will lift the back end up enough that it is not rubbing on the brake line. I will do it for $75 for you." I agreed, he fixed us up, and off we went.

We made it to Pueblo, Colorado, we still had over 100 miles to go. I was tired and hungry and could not go any further. I called my aunt to ask for her help. She said she would help me and told me to get some sleep. She paid for our motel that night. The next day, we finally arrived at her house in Denver. I only had $10 left in my pocket, but we made it! I know that the angels were watching over me and my children on that trip. We had too many close calls and avoided a disaster.

I stayed in Colorado for a few months but ended up going back to Arizona. The unemployment and job market in Colorado was terrible. I did manage to get a job in Pest Control for a few months, but trying to find affordable housing was difficult. I decided to go back to Arizona. John was still making it very difficult for me to see my son. The place I had been renting in Arizona when I left was available, and I had a part-time job waiting for me. I went back to Arizona for five more years. I went to college and got a job in the accounting field. After I finished college, I moved back to Colorado permanently. I was then able to move in with my Mom for a short time and then get my own place. I lived in a nice city and got an exceptionally good job with my accounting experience. I also got to see my middle son every other weekend - life was good. I eventually found Mile Hi Church and came to the end of my dark night of the soul journey.

I can say from my own experiences, that even in your darkest moments or most difficult times – have faith. You might find help from someone you know or even a stranger. Don't give up and believe that a higher power knows what you need and will be there. All you must do is ask and believe. Those darkest moments can define you and help you grow. Learn from them.

## Chapter 12
## The Power of Prayer and Faith

*I live in the faith that there is a Presence and Power greater than I am that nurtures and supports me in ways I could not even imagine. I know that this Presence is All knowing and All Power and is Always right where I am.*
*~Ernest Holmes*

I know firsthand the power of prayer and faith. I have found that prayer and faith can be a very important part to healing in many ways. I wanted to share some of my prayer and faith experiences with you.

When I went to church, I would see people healed by faith. At one point, when my daughter was about a year old, the doctors said she had asthma. I took her up to the front of the church during a service for a healing. Even though the minister never touched her, her asthma disappeared after that moment. She has never had any breathing disorders since.

I believed this healing happened because I was stepping out in faith and walked up to the front, seeking blessings and miracles. Like the story in the bible when the man came to Jesus to heal his sick servant.

Jesus said, take me to him. The man said "I believe you can heal him with your word, you need not go to him." Jesus said this man is a man of faith, and he said, "Go home, and you will find your servant healed," and he was. Matthew 8:5-13

Another time I found strong belief in prayer was on my daughter's first birthday. At her party, I told a group of people from the church that God would always take care of me and my children. At the time, the three of us were living with my sister and my father until I could find my own place. All of a sudden, there was a knock on the door. We were getting an eviction notice because we hadn't paid the full amount of the rent – only a partial amount. I had just told everyone, "God will always take care of me and my children," and then immediately received an eviction notice – how ironic this was.

I had no other choice except to have faith, so I did. The night before I was expected to be out, I still had not found a place to move into. Then I got a call from a man from our church, and he said, "I heard you were looking for a place to rent and for some reason, I don't even know why, but I bought a place, and if you want it, it's yours to rent, and I will give you a affordable monthly rate."

Wow! I stood in my faith and believed in what I needed to happen, and it happened. In the end, I got something even better than I could even have imagined.

Another time I stepped out in faith, we were strapped for money, and my daughter came home from 6th grade with a pamphlet about Sea Camp. She really wanted to go, but it was not in my budget to afford and send her to an expensive camp. I knew how good it would be for her and how much she would

## Chapter 12 - The Power of Prayer and Faith

love it. I signed the paper anyway. I decided to step out in faith and believe and pray that God would help me come up with the money for Sea Camp. Guess what?

The money I needed showed up in a very unexpected way. A man, I had just started dating, gave me the money so she could go to Sea Camp and later I paid him back in full.

I like to refer to having faith as "stepping out" in faith. As I mentioned before, *your thoughts can become things,* so you need to have positive thoughts when you step out in faith. Believe that what you want will happen. If you have doubts, it can keep things from manifesting in your life. Sometimes what we want is not necessarily what we should have, so the Universe may not manifest it. It may not be something good for us, even though we may want something in the moment. An example might be when we ask God or the Universe for a person we just met to be "the One."

And it doesn't work out, it was probably because it wasn't the right relationship for us. I don't know how many times I really wanted a certain person in my life only later to find out I was very glad that it didn't work out.

I have been driving for 40 years, and I have not been in any major car accidents. I went to see Deepak Chopra, who happened to be visiting our church. He said, "Why do some people never have car accidents, it is because it is not part of their reality." At that moment, I realized, what a concept that is. I remember when I worked in the mountains, some of the people I worked with were hitting deer regularly. They would joke, "I must be a deer magnet" well, I guess they made themselves what they said they were.

We create our own reality by our thoughts and words. We need to have positive words and thoughts if we want positive results in life. As an example, I was struggling in a new job as the workload was very far behind. It was very stressful, and I was not sure I wanted to stay. I decided to set an intention that this was going to be one of the best places I had ever worked. I wrote my intentions down, read them many times a day. I would close my eyes and imagine the intentions happening even though in that moment, they were not. Guess what? Eventually, it became one of the best places I have ever worked.

Regarding prayer, I have been attending prayer groups at my church. Each time, we set an intention for healing for someone in our group. We imagine bringing unconditional love from the source into our heart and then sending from the heart to the individual who needs the healing. What is interesting about this type of healing is that by sending this unconditional love and intention to someone, you are also receiving the healing as well.

I used to have a hard time with the concept of unconditional love and what it would feel like. I just thought about how much I love my children and pets, or how much my dog loves me – no matter what. That is what unconditional love is for me.

Think about what unconditional love means to you. Imagine if we sent this intention and unconditional love to every person we meet. Think how powerful it could be, to heal ourselves and those around us?

## Chapter 13
## An Interview with Courtney Smith:
## Tips on How to be Successful

*If you think you're to small to make a difference,
try sleeping with a mosquito in the room.
~ The Dalai Lama*

I wanted to add this interview to my book because I thought it was important to not only give you my thoughts about the body, mind, and spirit but also give you someone else's perspective and insight on being successful. Courtney Smith has become very successful in his life. He inspires me, and I hope you can use some of his tips to better your life.

Courtney Smith is a successful entrepreneur who I respect very much. I met Courtney by attending his stock trading classes. Courtney became successful from stock trading at a young age.

He now teaches students how to become successful stock traders. He owns a company called Wealth Builder. I was lucky enough to be able to interview him and get inside his head.

BL: I think a lot of people have the perception that if they become successful, they will become greedy and become a bad person. I know this is not true, but could you elaborate on this?

Courtney: Sure. You can rip off people, there is no question about that, but the problem is you can't make any sustainable money. You could rip people for a while, and then in some shape or form, you will get busted. Or nobody buys your product because it is a piece of garbage or whatever. There is another part - like what it does to the persons psychology. Those people are in a special kind of hell when they are ripping other people off. My motto in my company is "giving gets." We sit down and try to figure out how much we can give - that type of feeling is just good business. The more you give - the more you get back, and the more your business grows. When you talk about giving, we give of ourselves emotionally, and it is not always about material things, but people see the big heart my staff has for its customers. Most business owners sit around all day and obsess over what is it my customers want and what are they complaining about, and what can I do to make it better?

BL: In my book, I state if you want to change your life, you need to change your way of thinking. What thoughts might you give the average person that could help them think in more successful ways?

Courtney: As you focus on your life, you need to look at what is most important. In my business, I do trading, and I have a lot of losing trades. I've lost money on a million trades but also made money on a million trades, but so what? That is not what is important. I watched a guy lose all his money and net worth in just 3 and a half weeks. He was a professional poker player prior to becoming a trader, and he was very successful

## Chapter 13 - An Interview with Courtney Smith

at that. I watched him and was dumbfounded since he showed no signs of stress, and every day, he was happy go lucky. He was whistling, making jokes, and not one time did I see any stress on him. And I'll never forget this, it was in 1975, and I finally said to him, "how can you be so happy when you just got destroyed financially?" And he said, "Courtney... it ain't my life, it ain't my wife, it's just money, honey." I sat there and thought to myself - what he is saying is - there is nothing more precious than your life. You are nothing without that. The meaning of "it aint my wife" means he didn't lose someone he loved. He was attached to his life, and his love and everything else was not that important. So, I look at the same thing... like what is really important in your life and everything else really doesn't matter, so if I have a losing trade, who cares, it's just a losing trade.

You just need to keep the focus on what is really important, really deep down important, and that is your life and your love.

BL: When you first started trading and becoming successful, I'm sure you had a lot of challenges and setbacks. What did you do to overcome them, and what kept you from not giving up despite these setbacks?

Courtney: Part of it is related to the question I just answered. There have been periods of time in my life that I have been completely wiped out. I had nothing, but it has never really bothered me. It's just money honey, as my friend would say, and your self-worth is not your net worth, so that doesn't matter. The other thing I think, is never, never give up. If you know that what you're doing is right, then how can you possibly lose? Remember, it is not about the money. I'm fortunate to be a trader because, with trading, you can make a lot of money. It's not a job pumping gas. I don't have a career in a minimum wage business. But still, even if I did have a job making $10 an hour, the money is not the important thing; it's how you live your life. I would say understanding what is important, and if you understand what's important, it makes you calm-you don't panic anymore. So, you lose money. I lost $425,000 in 30 seconds, and it hurt for almost a full minute. But the point is-it's gone and now in the past-you must live in the now. Because as soon as you live in the now, there is no fear. If I live in the now, what are my fears? Maybe I'll lose all my money, but oh, I already lost it, so I need to focus on the now and the future, not the past. What can I learn from the past? I learned this lesson and this lesson - ok fine, - I don't have to think about the past anymore. It's over, no time to keep dragging it on. Everyone in this office will tell you I'm pretty relentless, that I never stop moving, I keep moving forward. I'm like a shark. A shark must keep moving forward in order to survive, and I'm like a shark in that way. It's a matter of keeping the focus on what is important. Once you know what is important, you live in the now. You can't feel fear, you can't feel anger, you can't feel any of these things because you now realize you need to just get on with what you need to do. One practical tip is people get overwhelmed when things go badly. So, you sit down and write what are the 10 things I need to do today, now cross off the 7 least important ones. Get the first 3 done, very few people can accomplish even the 3 things on the list. But you put them in order, and you don't go to number two until number one is done. Now suddenly you have direction in your life, but now all of sudden you have just lost $425,000 in 30 seconds-ok what do I do about it. I need to do this and do this, and now that I have focused, the emotions about losing the money are gone. Now I'm focused on what do I need to do to get the money back. By the way, in the end, I did get back the $425,000, so my whole month was a break-even. To start out the month with being out $425,000, and by the end of the month, I had it back and broke even-I was happy about that. And that was because I got back on the horse that threw me off.

## Chapter 13 - An Interview with Courtney Smith

BL: I find it interesting that you have talked about centering before you do any trading of a stock. Can you explain this a little more and how it could be beneficial in other areas of your life?

Courtney: Ok, let me expand on this. I meditated a lot when I was younger now I don't for the simple reason that I always feel calm. Let me give an example. I'm now 65 years old, and I have been a trader now for over 40 years. I speak on stages of as many as 1,000 to 5,000 people attending. I'll do this maybe 20 times a year. I fly all over the world and get jet lag that would be considered a very stressful life. So once a year I go in, and get blood tests done and the doctors cannot find any signs of stress. They don't find elevated cortisol levels, can't find any effect that I have too much adrenaline from my trading or public speaking. I don't want to say I'm a centered person. I'm a very calm person because of what I said before about what is really important. When I get on stage, do I know more than everyone else in the audience? Of course, I do. So why shouldn't I be confident? If I got on a stage with my peer group and they knew as much as I did - then maybe what I say could be right, or maybe I'm wrong. As long as my ego is not wrapped up into it, I'm ok. But if my ego gets wrapped into it, then I would start thinking about what if I'm wrong. I don't ever think about the word, it's about the action. I'm going to go out there and give the best speech I can, and then I may fail or I may succeed. But I will still give the best speech I possibly can. If I fail, I know I'm going to fail. As a trader, I have losing trades all the time, so it doesn't bother me. Because what am I going to do from a losing trade is learn something. My life would be better if I fail so I don't see the big problem of failing. I'm not afraid to fail at all. Why? Because I've done is so many times in my life, I'm used to it. To be a trader, you need to be humble, and the reason for that is because you have to do what the market tells you to do. When I'm trading and working, I have no ego at all.

I want to do the best job I possibly can. And that may mean I will succeed or that I may fail, but I know I did the best job I could, and that is the only thing in my control.

BL: I think fear is a big factor that keeps a lot of people stuck. We all have different fears, but could you give us some brief advice on overcoming some of the fears you have seen that have kept people from being successful?

Courtney: First off, you should never fear anything, you should never feel fear at all. And I'll give you two techniques right now for overcoming fear that you can use in any type of fear, like public speaking, or whatever it may be like you have got cancer. There are 2 things, first thing is educated action; fear is only of unknown things. We only fear the unknown. Let me give you an example, someone is worried that they will get cancer. That is about the future. Then they find out they have cancer. Are they worried about getting cancer anymore? No. They know they have cancer. Now they may be afraid to die. But do you see what I'm saying? When you have the fear of getting cancer, then you are fearful, and you are anxious. But once you get cancer, you are not fearful about getting cancer anymore because you now have it.

The first thing you need to do is educate yourself. What is it that you really fear? It may be jealousy, or you're worried your spouse is going to cheat on you? What could be the worst thing that would happen if that occurred. Live it in your mind, to find out what's really making you fearful. And educate yourself. Ask your wife or examine your own behavior. Maybe it is your fault. You can educate yourself in trading. For example – we have a series of losing trades - we then go back and see if there is something we did. We back test and look at our techniques, we can then see the technique constantly losing money. Then we shouldn't be using it. But if it has constantly made money in the past, but not right now, we should stick with it because it will come back into

# Chapter 13 - An Interview with Courtney Smith

a good system again. Once we educate ourselves, we think, ok I got it. The second thing is once you know the education is there, then you have to act. You will get a certain confidence in yourself by educating and then taking action. The next thing about fear is what we talked about already if you live in the now, there is no fear. Fear is about what could be, like I might get cancer, I might get hit by a truck; but if I'm in the now, like answering your questions, I won't be thinking about what could be.

BL: Is it something like when you look at the worst-case scenario of your wife cheating on you? You might think, ok, I'll get a divorce, and then after that, I'll be hurt and sad. But after that, what will happen in time is I will get better and will get on with my life. So, the worst-case scenario eventually works itself out.

Courtney: Yes, it is like I said, we educate ourselves. And then think about it, how many things are really worse than we think they will be? Hardly anything we are afraid of is not really as bad as we imagine them to be, you have already lived the worst-case scenario mentally before it has happened.

BL: The average person may see certain things too complicated to even try, and they might miss out on growing to their full potential. A good example would be trading. What advice might you tell that person?

Courtney: I'm a huge fan of simplification and everything we do in our company and everything I do in my life; I try to simplify. If we go back to cybernetics, simple systems are usually more robust. They live longer, they don't break down. I'm trained in computer science, and simple programs are better than complicated programs. I know, personally, I can tend to make things more complicated so I'm very overt on simplify, simplify. I'm relentlessly trying to cut things out of my life. I'm trying to reduce it by selling every object I own, so I don't own anything. I now live in hotels because I didn't want to own any objects at all.

Maybe that is a bizarre lifestyle, and maybe it won't work out, but I'm trying to cut out as many things as possible. That's freedom- cutting out all material things - they are of no real importance. We are sitting here on nice sofas and nice artwork on the walls; but I could get rid of it tomorrow, and that would be fine. If I simplify, it gives me less things to worry about. I'm a trader all day long. I'm trying to figure out ways to simplify. Can I cut out one step? This comes from my computer science background. The fewer steps I have, the more robust the system is. I'm always trying to simplify in everything. Things tend to grow over time. Like we hire too many people or have too many courses that we offer, or we have them in too many locations and then I have to say no. We need to simplify. Fewer courses in fewer locations and we will actually do better. We will stay very centered and less running around. What if we cut X out of our life, what would it mean? For example, what if you didn't watch TV. How much would you miss it? Start looking at your life and ask yourself, what if that wasn't there? I love to listen to Podcasts. I had 15 of them and some of these were an hour or more. I couldn't finish them during the day; I was always falling behind, so, I thought, ok, I listen to this one once a week so I will cut it out. That dress in your closet, you haven't worn in 3 years, do you really need that dress? The answer is clearly no, but if you think you are saving for a special occasion, then you can go out and buy a new one. Ask yourself the question, 'when was the last time I used that?' and think about maybe getting rid of it. Or what if I cut this out of my life – how much would I really miss it? What value is it bringing into my life? If I give up something in my life, I may get something even better to replace it. I sometimes cut things out of my life just to see what comes in. You need to open up some space for something new to come into your life.

## Chapter 13 - An Interview with Courtney Smith

BL: [Author and motivational speaker] T. Harv Eker says we should "practice happiness now." He said if you're not happy where you are right now, what makes you think you will be happy when you're rich? Would you mind elaborating on that statement and tell us what makes you happy?

Courtney: I agree 100%. Money doesn't buy happiness. I have been rich, and I have been poor, but rich is better. There is no doubt about that. But, once again, money is not that important, as we discussed earlier. It gives you more freedom to do more things at a higher level. And that is a good thing if you use money correctly, it is a very powerful tool. If you use it incorrectly, you're just a slave to money. As I mentioned to you at one time, I had the number one hedge fund, number one mutual fund, number one stock-picking letter, and number one picking futures letter all at the same time, but I was working 16 hours a day, 7 days a week. Was I making a lot of money? Sure…but did I have a life? My whole life was creating that track record, so who was in control of my life? Not me. The newsletter was in charge of my life, the mutual fund was in charge of my life, so I wasn't free.

I quit those things and shut them all down and said to myself, I need to get control of my life. It was a major changing point in my life. I enjoyed all that stuff, but when you do it 365 days out of the year, it becomes an obsession. Like T.Harv Eker says, practice happiness now, you don't need money to be happy. You can enjoy sitting in the sun, and you don't have to be rich to enjoy it. I like having money better than not having money, but you can still be happy. I think the happier you are – the more money you'll make.

People are attracted to people that are happy. Who wants to do business with a grouch? Happiness and freedom have to come before the money. I may have to end a business relationship, and I may make less money, but I won't have to deal with people I don't enjoy dealing with. You need to cut out the things in your life that make you unhappy. When I do, I will be happier and probably make more money by doing that. Everybody is afraid to give up the money, but you will get it back and be happier. How can you do good work if you're miserable? Find something that you enjoy more.

*If you are interested in getting to know more about Courtney, please go to wealthbuilderllc.com or courtneysmith.com.*

## Chapter 14
## Meditation: My Healing
### of the Body Meditation

I wanted to conclude this book with a meditation that you can follow along with. Before you begin a meditation, find a place that is quiet and has no distractions. The best place is a room where you can close the door–so you will not be disturbed. Try to take at least 10 to 20 minutes to meditate, the longer the better. You can do it sitting up or laying down. If you fall asleep during your meditation, that is okay, your body needed it. You may want to set a timer.

I understand that reading and meditating are hard to do at the same time. After you read this a few times, you can improvise and say the words in your head or out loud. The exact words are not important. Like I tell my students in my T'ai Chi class–it is not about perfection but intention. You can also record the following meditation on your phone and then play it to yourself.

Close your eyes… and take a deep breath in… and slowly exhale… take another deep breath in… and slowly exhale… feeling your body relax… with each breath you feel more relaxed... relaxing your neck and shoulders... all the tension leaves... relaxing your arms... feeling your stomach muscles and lower back relaxing... your legs feel light... your whole body is now relaxed and all tension is gone.... you feel like your floating on warm water....

I want you to imagine a bright golden light coming down from the universe and entering the top of your head... this is a warm and healing golden light... as the light enters your head it glows with a warm healing light... the glowing light slowly moves down into your brain and sinus cavities and ears... imagine each cell is being healed and renewed by this light...

It moves down your throat... and into your spine... as the light moves down your spine, imagine it is healing every cell in your body... your upper torso and all the internal organs are now glowing with this golden light... all your organs are being rejuvenated and healed by this golden light...

Your body feels warm and comfortable... your arms and hands and all the muscles and joints in your body is being healed... you see and feel this healing light moving through your body... every cell is being renewed and healed... imagine the light moving down through your lower torso and into your legs... every muscle and joint... your hips and knees feel renewed...

It's moving down your calves and shins and into your feet... your whole entire body is immersed in this golden light... all your cells are smiling...

You feel warm and wonderful all over... knowing that this light is healing and rejuvenating each and every cell... feel the serenity of this moment as you see your whole body glowing with this healing light (pause) imagine the tips of your toes and fingers opening as the light passes out through your toes and fingertips and into the ground... the light is taking all toxins with it into the ground where mother nature will then filter it and change it into good energy...

## Chapter 14 - Meditation

Feeling the new you in this moment (pause) you slowly become aware of the room around you...and when you're ready you can open your eyes... and you will feel totally renewed and healed.

I'm planning soon to record a guided meditation CD, but my intention was to write this book first. Be on the lookout for my Healing Meditations CD for more meditations that you can follow from home.

I hope you enjoyed my book and was able to get some ideas and insight on things. I know that everything may have not resonated with you. Things I said may have not been what you believe in - so take what works for you and disregard what doesn't.

My intention is to help people and if this book helps just one person, I have accomplished my goal. Sending love and blessings to you all.

*The best and most beautiful things in this world
cannot be seen or even heard but must be felt with the heart.
-Hellen Keller*

www.ingramcontent.com/pod-product-compliance
Lightning Source LLC
Chambersburg PA
CBHW071410290426
44108CB00014B/1761